I0756812

HEALTHCARE IN PRACTICE

COMMUNICATING PRINCIPLES OF
PRACTICE IN HEALTH AND SOCIAL CARE

OGUCHI MARTINS EGBUJOR

authorHOUSE

AuthorHouse™ UK
1663 Liberty Drive
Bloomington, IN 47403 USA
www.authorhouse.co.uk
Phone: UK TFN: 0800 0148641 (Toll Free inside the UK)
        UK Local: 02036 956322 (+44 20 3695 6322 from outside the UK)

© 2020 OGUCHI MARTINS EGBUJOR. All rights reserved.

No part of this book may be reproduced, stored in a retrieval system, or
transmitted by any means without the written permission of the author.

Published by AuthorHouse 10/15/2020

ISBN: 978-1-7283-5657-0 (sc)
ISBN: 978-1-7283-5658-7 (hc)
ISBN: 978-1-7283-5659-4 (e)

Print information available on the last page.

Any people depicted in stock imagery provided by Getty Images are models,
and such images are being used for illustrative purposes only.
Certain stock imagery © Getty Images.

This book is printed on acid-free paper.

Because of the dynamic nature of the Internet, any web addresses or links contained in
this book may have changed since publication and may no longer be valid. The views
expressed in this work are solely those of the author and do not necessarily reflect the
views of the publisher, and the publisher hereby disclaims any responsibility for them.

About the Author

Oguchi Martins Egbujor FCMI is a UK based Lecturer in Business and Management, and Health and Social Care. Oguchi has over ten years of teaching and assessment experience. He had taught in various programmes relating to Business Management and Health and Social Care from BTEC HND to BA Business and Management. Oguchi specializes in Strategic Management and Strategic

Human Resource Management though he teaches other business subjects effectively. Oguchi Martins Egbujor is a contributor to international issues concerning the education and development of mankind.

Contents

The Communication Boundary

Communication in this book is relating to healthcare professional-patient relationship as described by the Health and Social Care Act 2008 (Regulated Activities) regulations 2014, and to be focused on achieving the fundamental purpose of communicating in healthcare sector. It is essential to set the context in which this book is written. Communication as mentioned in this book is that which is carried out by the following:

- ➢ Healthcare professional means a person who is registered as a member of any profession to which section 60 (2) of the Health Act 1999 (13) (regulation of health professions, social workers, other care workers, etc) applies.
- ➢ Personal care means physical assistance given to a person in connection with:-

1. eating or drinking (including the maintenance of established parenteral nutrition)

2. toileting (including in relation to the process of menstruation)
3. washing or bathing
4. dressing
5. oral care
6. the skin, hair and nails (with the exception of nail care provided by a chiropodist or podiatrist)

It is therefore, obvious that Communication in this book is any interrelationship and interaction taking place within the context and environment as described above.

Purpose of Communication in Healthcare Sector

The purpose of communication in healthcare sector is to create understanding between care provider and the care receiver. That is the care professionals and their clients that include the patients, family, friends and their well-wishers. In communication of any kind, the aim is to send a message that is clear, concise and understood by the receiver.

Communication in healthcare is a sensitive issue and the communicators should be polite, empathise and be sympathetic with the healthcare receiver. Whoever comes in contact with a doctor, a nurse and/or a care practitioner officially is to inquire about the welfare of either for himself or herself and for that of others. Therefore, a care giver should be able to be sensitive and sympathetic to their cause. At the heart of healthcare communication are confidentiality, trust, respect and reassurance, even in the face of difficulties. This system of communication builds a good relationship between the communicator and the receiver. The importance of communication in health and social care cannot be over-emphasised as all the fundamental practices of health and social care are dependent on it. All healthcare practitioners discharge their duties based on their code of practice which relies on effective communication.

Communicating to Develop Understanding

Communicating Effectively

According to National Institute of Clinical Excellence (NICE), patients experience effective interactions with staff who have demonstrated competency in relevant communication skills. Communication being the imparting or exchanging of information by speaking, writing and/or using other forms of interaction is to convey a coded message to the receiver with an intention that it will be interpreted appropriately and understood as the sender intended.

Trust is the key in healthcare sector, and patients look up to the professionals to maintain confidentiality in communication. Patients look up to professionals who listen to understand their needs. Understanding patient's needs is critical in offering good service.

However effective communication must be:

> ➢ Clear
> ➢ Simple and short
> ➢ Addressing the needs
> ➢ Reassuring patients
> ➢ Relevant to the patient's needs
> ➢ Delivering intended outcomes

The purpose of communication in healthcare sector is also to inform patients of their right; inform professionals and providers of the guiding principles and expectations of the government and regulators so as to achieve quality service and customer satisfaction. The purpose of communication is not achieved without quality service and the satisfaction of patients on the services received from professionals.

Verbal communication and non-verbal communication through observation of body languages are critical in professionals performing their duties. In this case, communication is putting into practice all the rules and regulations guiding healthcare profession. Performing any activity in healthcare industry is termed to be "communication" as the observer takes note mentally and assesses whether it is carried out rightly or wrongly.

Practically doing one's work without saying anything is also a direct communication to the observer as body language is called into action. A patient observing a healthcare practitioner may understand when something is not going right. For example:

- ❖ A nurse who is not comfortable with needle/ injection
- ❖ A carer who cannot understand patient's medication

❖ A doctor who does not understand the result of a test

❖ A manager who cannot interpret new policies

❖ A professional who is confused

❖ A practitioner who may not understand his or her duties and responsibilities.

Building Good Relationship

Demonstrating good understanding and using the right skills communicates proficiency or competency to the patient who is either interacting verbally or non-verbally with a practitioner. The purpose of communication is therefore, to pass on a message from one person to the other with the intention of building an understanding.

The characteristics of patient-practitioner relationship are:

- Communication builds understanding
- Understanding builds trust.
- Trust builds confidence.
- Confidence builds assurance.
- Assurance builds satisfaction.
- Satisfaction builds good relationship

Patient-Practitioner Relationship

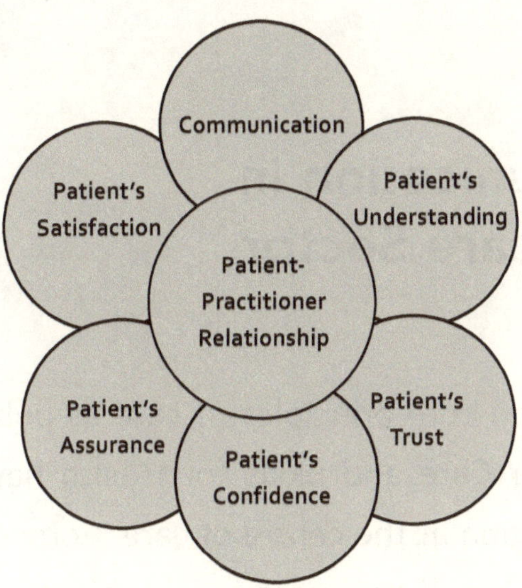

Patient Satisfaction is therefore, the achievement of intended outcomes. The combination of the above characteristics builds good relationship between patients and healthcare professionals.

Communication in Healthcare Sector

The common core principles of care as published 2015 by Skills for Care and Skills for Health have effective communication at the centre of care. Communication in this book is based on professional-patient interaction as set out by Department of Health (DoH) United Kingdom. The aim of this book is to achieve customer satisfaction as prescribed in the Health and Social Care Act 2008 (Regulated Activities) Regulations 2014. Communication in healthcare industry is person-centred and this approach governs the tenets of quality care. There are person-centred values that must be followed to achieve positive result in healthcare. These values are:

> Individuality
> Independence
> Dignity
> Privacy
> Respect

- ➢ Trust
- ➢ Choice
- ➢ Partnership

The applications of the above values ensure good practice and patient satisfaction. All the communications and applications of rules and regulations must revolve around these values of person-centred approach.

Dignity and Respect

How Does Communication Work In Practice

Communication is the interaction between two or more people. In other words, communication is the transmission of an idea to another person for the purpose of creating an understanding. In this case, communication is between:

> - healthcare provider and the patient
> - healthcare provider and the patient's relatives
> - healthcare provider and their workforce
> - Healthcare provider and other partners
> - healthcare provider and the governing bodies

Communication is about forming an idea and passing it on to someone else with the aim of creating an understanding. For communication to take place there is a process of forming an idea (mentally), encoding an idea, and sending out the coded idea. Communication can be turned into noise or distorted at this stage due to the processes either the mode or channel by which it is sent. The mode or channel must be known and understandable by the intended person, the receiver.

The circumstances of the receiver (patient) must be put into consideration. The sending of an encoded message must be received by the intended person, and he, she or they have to decode it or interpreting it meaningfully. Any Message must be understood for it to be deemed received. Communication could be verbal or non-verbal. The utterances and the body language are all part of sending messages to the receiver. However, if any (utterance or body language) is not composed properly, it may send out a wrong message. In that case, such communication is nothing but noise if not understood by the receiver.

However when a message is received and understood, it triggers response. Response can be positive or negative. Communication is therefore, between sender and receiver, and it must create an understanding. The question then becomes "what is the intention" of the sender? It must be:

- To establish dialogue
- To inform the patient
- To inform the patient's relatives
- To inform colleagues
- To inform employer or employee
- To inform partners
- To inform the governing bodies, etc.

Principles of Care

According to the principles of care, as published by Skills for Care and Skills for Health in 2015, effective communication is an essential part of care and therefore, should be:

- ➢ Non-judgemental
- ➢ Empathetic
- ➢ Supportive
- ➢ Genuine and authentic
- ➢ Collaborative

Communication in healthcare sector does not necessarily mean talking to or talking at someone. It is a holistic process of understanding and satisfying individual's needs without prejudice. This means that to achieve customer satisfaction in care, care providers must not be judgemental. They must interact with their service users with open mind, showing empathy and genuineness. To meet a patient's needs, there must be a collaborative working, involving other partners to achieve a patient-centred outcome of the care plan.

Forms of Communication

What Message Are You Sending?

There are two forms of communication, namely:

- ➤ Verbal
- ➤ Non-verbal

These two forms of communication are used on a daily basis. They are intertwined and inextricable. They are used simultaneously. Verbal and non-verbal communications are consciously and unconsciously practised. One cannot listen to any verbal communication without observing the body language of the communicator.

Verbal Communication

Verbal communication is an interaction between two or more people by the use of sound, spoken through word of mouth. It is an audible interaction where the sender uses sound or pronouncement by the use of voice, such as talking, whistling, groaning, yelling and others. The sound made is intended for someone to hear and understand it, otherwise, it is classified as noise. It is the system of communication that requires the mouth and the ear.

The mouth is the sender and the ear is the receiver. The sender must be audible enough for the sound to travel the distance to the receiver who lends his ears to receive it. The sound must be decoded or interpreted into message by the receiver to be able to understand its' meaning.

Understanding the decoded message will lead to positive or negative reaction by the receiver. Usually, the intention of the encoder is to create positive reaction however, it is not always the case as some messages are understood according to the interpretation of the message by the receiver. In some cases, the communication maybe deemed ineffective. For communication to be effective, it must be concise and focused. The message must be relevant and timely otherwise it becomes offensive. The right message must be sent at the right time. A message must be concrete and with a purpose. The purpose must be relevant to the receiver.

Non-verbal Communication

Non-verbal communication is the opposite of verbal communication, it is not spoken. Non-verbal communication is an interaction between two or more people by the use of body language. As usual, it is also involved sender and receiver of a message. One sends a message to the receiver by movement of the body termed signal. Like verbal communication, messages by signs are also encoded and it is the responsibility of the receiver to decode or interpret it into meaning. The sender must ensure that the signal he or she sends is intended to communicate a positive message otherwise it could be interpreted to cause an offence. The body movements may be by:

- ➢ Nodding the head,
- ➢ Shaking the head,
- ➢ Winking or starring of the eyes,
- ➢ Contrasting or contracting the face (frowning or smiling),
- ➢ Uprightly raising the palm or the thumb
- ➢ Waving the hand
- ➢ Giving a thumb up or thumb down
- ➢ Positioning the fingers over the ear (sign of telephone)

➢ Pulling ear slightly down
➢ Using other known communication signs (sign languages)
➢ Shaking the legs and many more and others

Unlike the verbal communication, the sender makes a body movement or sign and the receiver has to observe and recognise the body movement or sign to be able to decode or interpret it so as to understand it. As the receiver listens in verbal communication, he, she or they must pay attention to be able to observe and understand non-verbal communication. The receiver of verbal communication must listen to the sound and the receiver of non-verbal communication must observe the body language. In healthcare industry, the care giver must understand both forms of communication.

Types of Communication

> ➢ Spoken Communication
>
> ➢ Written Communication
>
> ➢ Visual Communication
>
> ➢ Signal Communication
>
> ➢ Audio Communication
>
> ➢ Sign Language Communication
>
> ➢ Social Media Communication
>
> ➢ Mass Media Communication and many more.

In healthcare industry, it is advisable to use the right type of communication to be able to communicate effectively with patients or clients. One also needs to use the right mode or form of communication in order to build good relationship with clients or patients. Communication is central to any organisation's success. Developing the right skills will help practitioners to build or mend bridges with their clients or patients.

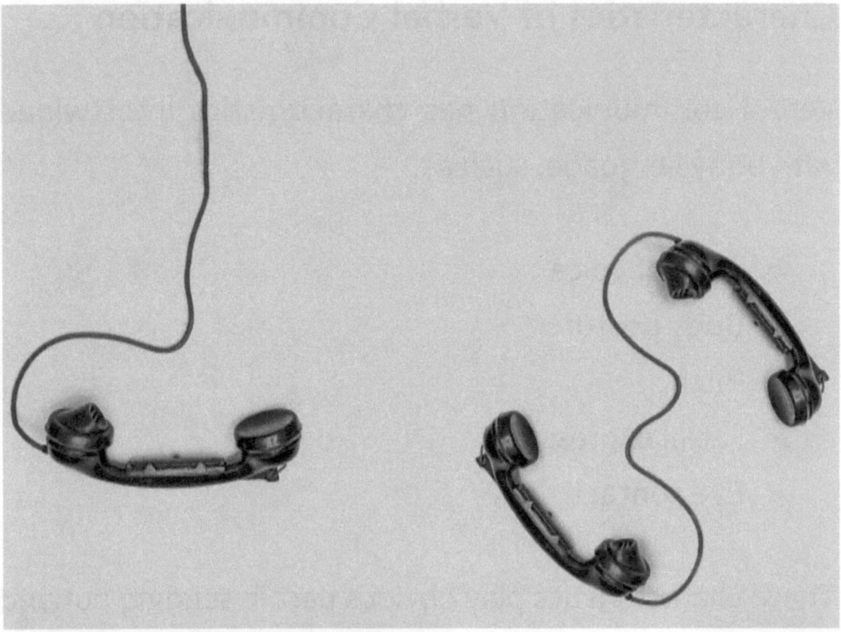

Creating and developing understanding in various ways

Characteristics of Verbal Communication

Verbal communication has characteristics intertwined with body language, such as:

> ➤ Tone of voice
> ➤ Body posture
> ➤ Pitch,
> ➤ Facial expression,
> ➤ Eye contact.

These characteristics play obvious part in sending out and receiving messages. These characteristics contribute to a message being viewed as positive or negative. The tone of voice, facial expression and eye contact are decoded along with the spoken words. The combination makes a message clearer to the recipient. The clarity may be positive, as well as negative. Most of the intentions of verbal communication are conveyed by its characteristics. The receiver observes and decodes inclusively the spoken words and the body language, so as to discern the true meaning of the message. To be mindfully aware of the characteristics of verbal communication will help the sender to achieve its intention. There are also other characteristics that contribute to the understanding of a message or lack of it. The Cobweb of Messaging needs to be effectively decoded.

To pass the message across you do not need to shout

The Cobweb of Messaging

These are a holistic signals and sounds intertwined as a message received as the intentions of the sender that need to be discerned (decoded) for a true meaning, positive or negative.

Discerning the Cobweb of Messaging
(Verbal and Non-verbal)

Environmental Characteristics of Communication

The environment plays a vital role in ensuring effective communication. In healthcare industry, the physical condition of the place of communication is important as it contributes to the intention of the sender. Trust and confidence are gained or lost due to the environment. The environment includes:

- ➤ Noise
- ➤ Lighting
- ➤ Proximity
- ➤ Sitting arrangement
- ➤ Temperature of the room
- ➤ Colour
- ➤ location
- ➤ Size
- ➤ Surroundings
- ➤ Timing
- ➤ State of mind, and many more.

These environmental characteristics play important roles in verbal communication, especially, one-to-one with patients and clients. Healthcare workers must be mindful of the environment of the location where communication is taking place. The environment may be intimidating to a patient or it may be shabby to demonstrate contempt to the patient.

Environmental State of Mind

The characteristics of environment state of mind may include:

> Emotion
> Stress
> Fear
> Anxiety
> Wellbeing

Any of these characteristics are not spoken, concealed and person. The effectiveness of any communication depends on the environmental state of mind of the sender and that of the receiver. This factor obscures any messages on either side and can lead to a dense cobweb of messaging. Prior to commencing a communication, it is advisable to review the environmental state of mind of the receiver otherwise a good message with good intention may be received negatively. Healthcare professionals must be mindful of this factor hence the message should be short, simple and focused to the point.

Environmental Mindset

Techniques for One-on-One Communication

There are various techniques for one-on-one communication. However, two techniques are more recognisable in healthcare communication than others, namely:

> ➢ SOLER technique (by Gerard Egan)
> ➢ EARS technique

There is also a newly developed techniques that is designed to assist care workers in achieving effective communication

> ➢ **SPRINKLE** techniques

These three techniques help healthcare providers to communication effectively with their patients or clients. To understand the techniques, one needs to understand the acronyms as follows:

SOLER

- ❖ S stands for **Sit upright**
- ❖ O stands for **Open mind**
- ❖ L stands for **Lean forward**
- ❖ E stands for **Eye contact**
- ❖ R stands for **Relaxation**

EARS

- ❖ E stands for **Explore** by asking open questions
- ❖ A stands for **Affirm** to show that you are listening
- ❖ R stands for **Reflect** your understanding
- ❖ S stands for **Silence** attentively

SPRINKLE

- ❖ S stands for **Soothing** words
- ❖ P stands for **Passionate** by demonstrating professionalism
- ❖ R stands for **Relate/Reassuringly** with the speaker to create trust
- ❖ I stands for **Interruption** by focusing on the points without interrupting
- ❖ N stands for **Neutrality** by maintaining an open mind
- ❖ K stand **Kindness** by empathy
- ❖ L stands for **Lead** by doing the right thing
- ❖ E stands for **Enthusiasm** by being cheerful and show interest in the topic

In the next chapter, the use of these techniques and skills will be used to form effective communication needed in healthcare sector.

Communication Skills

Communication skill is the acquisition or the development of human ability and capability that enables one to engage in conversation with other people to achieve a common understanding between the sender and the receiver. This involves the ability to co-operate with others. Communication skills help to create trust and good relationship. These skills involve:

- ➢ Co-operation
- ➢ Enthusiasm
- ➢ Listening
- ➢ Attentive
- ➢ Articulation
- ➢ Observation
- ➢ Empathy
- ➢ Controlled-Emotion
- ➢ Retentive
- ➢ Initiative
- ➢ Rephrasing
- ➢ Recapitulation
- ➢ Reflecting
- ➢ Summarising
- ➢ Leadership

Anyone who has acquired all these communication skills will excel in his profession. He or she is gifted. Patients and colleague will respect him. He will make friends wherever he or she goes. Patients and clients will want to interact with him as they take him as 'one-of-us' and relate with him easily. Any healthcare provider who possesses these skills will maintain peace, convince people with ease, create supportive environment and satisfy his customers. Patients will confide in him, and he will be seen as an action oriented person. His or her response to any issue will be soothing, healing and supportive. Patients view any professional with these skills as intelligent, gifted and matured to handle their affairs to their satisfaction.

Barrier to Communication

Communication barriers are any items or issues, in other words "factors" that may distort a message, thereby, preventing it to be understood as intended by the sender, be it physical or sensory disturbance that interferes with the transmission of the message. Communication barrier is any activity that may obstruct the passage of a coded message therefore, rendering it distorted, incomplete, or misunderstood by the receiver.

In healthcare provision, barriers to communication may be:

- Language
- Culture
- Emotional
- Timing
- Interruption
- Impatience
- Location
- Channel of communication
- Technology
- Disability
- Noise
- Visibility
- Accent

- Stereo-typing
- Assumption
- Proximity
- Misinterpretation
- Ambiguity
- Body language
- Tone of voice
- Trust
- Confidence
- Pronunciation
- Jargon
- Slangs

THE COBWEB OF MESSAGING

- ✓ Timing
- ✓ State of Mind
- ✓ Language
- ✓ Jargon
- ✓ Body Language
- ✓ Tone of Voice
- ✓ Stereo-typing
- ✓ Mode of communication
- ✓ Channel of communication
- ✓ Trust and confidentiality
- ✓ Ambiguity of words
- ✓ Encoding format
- ✓ Decoding format
- ✓ Misinterpretation
- ✓ Pronunciation
- ✓ Lighting
- ✓ Location
- ✓ Circumstances surrounding patient's illness
- ✓ Positive and Negative Signals
- ✓ Pre-emption of notion
- ✓ Treatment reaction of patient's health or illness

Environment may be intimidating and distracting to a patient. The list of barriers is endless. Healthcare practitioner must evaluate any of the above issues according to the needs of a patient. People tend to ignore emotional barriers. Surrounding healthcare practice is the emotion of a patient. The environment also constitutes a barrier. Being in hospital environment may be intimidating to a patient, and may also send a wrong signal. Some people experience high blood pressure or stress by just simply being near a hospital or in the care home. Another barrier to note is assumption. Practitioners may assume that a patient is well informed but that may not be true. Encoding of a message plays critical part in understanding of a message. By assumption, a practitioner encodes a message, believing that the patient understands it, when the receiver has no clue as to what the words, abbreviation or acronyms means. The healthcare practitioner must acquire appropriate interpersonal communication skills

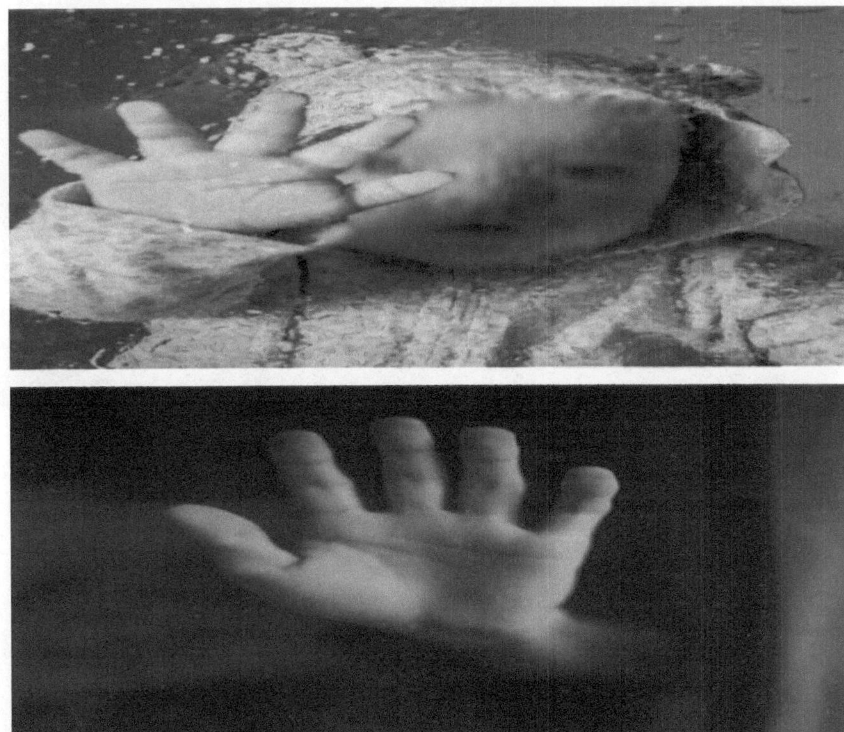

Barriers of Communication

Interpersonal Communication Skills

Interpersonal communication skill is the ability and capability of a healthcare worker or practitioner to interrelate with service users, so as to create rapport, maintain trust and confidence, and to build good relationship for the satisfaction of their service users. Lack of interpersonal communication skills leads to barriers and inappropriate communication. A healthcare practitioner must ensure that he or she eliminates all the barriers as listed above to be able to interact effectively with the service users, their relatives and the colleagues. In healthcare industry, inappropriate communication must be eliminated to ensure that messages are received and understood as the sender intended. Effective communication in healthcare provision is to deliver services as the government and regulators intended to achieve customer satisfaction. Understanding the principles of practice in healthcare sector is paramount to good service.

Ineffective Communication

Principles Enabling Communication in Healthcare Provision

According to Nursing and Midwifery Council (NMC) 2015, the fundamentals of care include, but are not limited to, nutrition, hydration, bladder and bowel care, physical handling and making sure that those receiving care are kept in clean and hygienic conditions. It includes making sure that those receiving care have adequate access to nutrition and hydration, and making sure that you provide help to those who are not able to feed themselves or drink fluid unaided.

However on the other hand, principle may be described as a fundamental truth or proposition that serves as the foundation for a system of belief or behaviour or for a chain of reasoning. Principle is a basic idea or rule that explains or controls how something happens or works.

Principles of communication in healthcare provision are therefore, those basic rules as established by the government and the governing bodies such as Care Quality Commission, National Institute for Clinical Excellence, British Medical Council, Nursing and Midwifery Council, etc., for the care and treatment of a patient or service user. These principles are set out in legislations, policies and regulations as guiding basic rules to achieve efficiency and customer satisfaction in healthcare industry. Practising one's profession according to the basic principles leads to proficiency. The first basic rule to professional competency in healthcare sector is to communicate the principles of practice in accordance with one's profession.

Standard Practices in Health and Social Care
are guided by Law, Rules and Regulations for
Quality Assurance and Customer Satisfaction

Principles and code of Practice in Healthcare Sector

There are different professions in healthcare sector. Each profession has its principles guiding it. To achieve the aim of this book is to focus on those front line services that affect the life of a patient, such as doctors, nurses, pharmacists, physiotherapists, nutritionists, carers and other associated employees and employers. There are codes of practice to guide all those involved in ensuring patient's welfare.

Code of Practice for Doctors in England

The British Medical Council is the regulating body for medical doctors in England. This body periodically reviews its code of practice through a framework. The good medical practice framework for appraisal and revalidation, published in 2013 as a review for the framework set out in 2011, outlined the framework in four (4) domains:

> - Knowledge, Skill and Performance
> - Safety and Quality
> - Communication, Partnership and Teamwork
> - Maintaining Trust

Domain 1.1 states that doctors must maintain their professional performance:

- ❖ Maintain knowledge of the law and other regulation relevant to their work
- ❖ Keep knowledge and skills about their current work up to date
- ❖ Participate in professional development and educational activities
- ❖ Take part in and respond constructively to the outcome of systematic quality improvement

activities (eg audit), appraisals and performance review

Domain 2.1 states that doctors must contribute to and comply with systems to protect patients

- ✓ Take part in systems of quality assurance and quality improvement
- ✓ Comply with risk management and clinical governance procedures
- ✓ Co-operate with legitimate requests for information from organisations monitoring public health
- ✓ Provide information for confidential inquiries, significant event reporting
- ✓ Make sure that all staff for whose performance you are responsible, including locums and students, are properly supervised
- ✓ Report suspected adverse reactions
- ✓ Ensure arrangements are made for the continuing care of the patient where necessary
- ✓ Ensure systems are in place for colleagues to raise concerns about risks to patients

Domain 3.1 states that doctors must communicate effectively

1. Listen to patients and respect their views about their health
2. Give patients the information they need in order to make decisions about their care in a way they can understand
3. Respond to patients' questions
4. Keep patients informed about the progress of their care
5. Explain to patients when something has gone wrong
6. Treat those close to the patient considerately
7. Communicate effectively with colleagues within and outside the team
8. Encourage colleagues to contribute to discussions and to communicate effectively with each other
9. Pass on information to colleagues involved in, or taking over, your patients' care

Domain 4.1 states that doctors must show respect for patients

- Implement and comply with systems to protect patient confidentiality

- Be polite, considerate and honest and respect patients' dignity and privacy
- Treat each patient fairly and as an individual
- If you undertake research, respect the rights of patients participating in the research

For the purpose of this book, this passage will be focusing on domain 2 and 3 and vaguely touched on the others to drum home the purpose of communication in healthcare provision. As domain 2 (two) demands, medical doctors must comply with the systems to protect patients; and domain 3 (three) demands effective communication by medical doctors. The 'systems' is a reference to all the basic rules and regulations guiding the medical practice and it is intertwined with communication. The combination of the two principles produces customer satisfaction. The rest of the framework is published as an appendix.

Code of Practice for Nursing and Midwifery

The Nursing and Midwifery Council (NMC) is the regulating body for nurses and midwives in England. On the 29th January, 2015, the NMC published a new code of professional practice for nurses and midwives, effective 31st March, 2015. The code of practice has twenty five (25) principles introduced in four (4) domains:

> - Prioritise People
> - Practise Effectively
> - Preserve Safety
> - Promote Professionalism and Trust

To briefly explain these principles under each domain, see as identified below:

Prioritise People

1. Treat people as individuals and uphold their dignity
2. Listen to people and respond to their preferences and concerns
3. Make sure that people's physical, social and psychological needs are assessed and responded to
4. Act in the best interests of people at all times
5. Respect people's right to privacy and confidentiality

Practice Effectively

6. Always practise in line with the best available evidence
7. Communicate clearly
8. Work co-operatively
9. Share your skills, knowledge and experience for the benefit of people receiving care and your colleagues
10. Keep clear and accurate records relevant to your practice
11. Be accountable for your decisions to delegate tasks and duties to other people
12. Have in place an indemnity arrangement which provides appropriate cover for any practice you take on as a nurse or midwife in the United Kingdom

Preserve Safety

13. Recognise and work within the limits of your competence
14. Be open and candid with all service users about all aspects of care and treatment, including when any mistakes or harm have taken place

15. Always offer help if an emergency arises in your practice setting or anywhere else
16. Act without delay if you believe that there is a risk to patient safety or public protection
17. Raise concerns immediately if you believe a person is vulnerable or at risk and needs extra support and protection
18. Advise on, prescribe, supply, dispense or administer medicines within the limits of your training and competence, the law, our guidance and other relevant policies, guidance and regulations
19. Be aware of, and reduce as far as possible. any potential for harm associated with your practice

Promote Professionalism and Trust

20. Uphold the reputation of your profession at all times
21. Uphold your position as a registered nurse or midwife
22. Fulfil all registration requirements
23. Cooperate with all investigations and audits
24. Respond to any complaints made against you professionally

25. Provide leadership to make sure that people's wellbeing is protected and to improve their experiences of the healthcare system

Nutrition

Code of Conduct for Healthcare Support Workers and Adult Social Care Workers

To understand the differences between healthcare support worker and the adult social care worker, the Department of Health set the definition as follows:

Healthcare Support Worker (including an Assistant Practitioner) in England who reports to a Registered Nurse or Midwife. Healthcare Support Workers reporting to other healthcare professionals are not currently included.

Adult Social Care Worker in England, this could either be in an independent capacity (for example, as a Personal Assistant); for a residential care provider; or as a supported living, day support or domiciliary care worker. The Code does not apply to Social Work Assistants.

To achieve wellbeing of patients or service users, there is collaboration between medical doctor, nurses, social care and support workers. To maintain good practice in the provision of healthcare, the Skills for Care in 2013 assumed the responsibilities of General Social Care Council. Skills for Care, funded by the Department of Health, in 2013 introduced a revised code of practice for healthcare workers.

There are therefore, seven principles guiding the code of practice for healthcare support workers, and health and social care workers:

> Be accountable by making sure you can answer for your actions or omissions
> Promote and uphold the privacy, dignity, rights, health and wellbeing of people who use healthcare services at all times
> Work in collaboration with your colleagues to ensure the delivery of high quality, safe and compassionate healthcare, care and support
> Communicate in an open and effective way to promote the health, safety and wellbeing of people who use health and care services and their carers
> Respect people's right to confidentiality
> Strive to improve the quality of healthcare, care and support through continuing professional development
> Uphold and promote equality, diversity and inclusion

The Rules and Regulations Guiding Healthcare Sector

By 1st of April 2015, the Health and Social Care Act 2008 (Regulated Activities) Regulations 2014 became effective. These regulations set out a new framework for care standard in England. The government of United Kingdom responding to the recommendations of various commissioned inquiries, reviews, consultations, and policy initiatives such as:

> ➢ Sir Francis Report 2013,
> ➢ The Winterbourne View Review 2013,
> ➢ The Berwick Review 2013
> ➢ The government Red Tape challenges

The government consulted with CQC and care users to set a new care standard framework. The Health and Social Care Act 2008 (Regulated Activities) Regulations 2014 as amended came into effect for hospital on the 1st of October, 2014. This set new powers for Care Quality Commission to encourage a culture of openness and to hold care providers and directors to account. The new frameworks came in five domains, namely:

- ➢ Safety
- ➢ Effectiveness
- ➢ Responsiveness
- ➢ Caring
- ➢ Well-led

Understand the rules and regulations
guiding your practice

The Key Lines of Enquiries (KLOE)

Safe	By safe, we mean that people are protected from abuse and avoidable harm.
Effective	By effective, we mean that people's care, treatment and support achieves good outcomes, promotes a good quality of life and is evidence-based where possible.
Caring	By caring, we mean that staff involve and treat people with compassion, kindness, dignity and respect.
Responsive	By responsive, we mean that services are organised so that they meet people's needs.
Well-led	By well-led we mean that the leadership, management and governance of the organisation assures the delivery of high-quality person-centred care, supports learning and innovation, and promotes an open and fair culture.

David Behan, the chief executive of Care Quality Commission (CQC) stated that "new regulations setting out fundamental standards of quality and safety now enable us to move to the next stage of development. The regulations are called the Health and Social Care Act 2008 (Regulated Activities) Regulations 2014. They are more focused than the previous ones. They will enable us to pinpoint more clearly the standards below which care must not fall, and take appropriate enforcement action, in line with Sir Robert Francis's recommendations arising from his inquiry into care at Mid-Staffordshire NHS Foundation Trust."

The Five Domains of fundamental standards as explained by CQC:

Is this service safe?

❖ In adult social care, safety has to be balanced with people's right to make choices and take risks. Our standards and the information we use will need to be clear that this balance is important. We also need to recognise the important role of safeguarding as a key aspect of safety in this sector.

Is this service effective?

❖ In adult social care being effective is about how services help people to live their lives in the way they choose and be as independent as possible – a key aspect of personalisation. Personalised care may look different for a 28-year old disabled person and a 90-year old person with dementia. We recognise that defining effective outcomes is one of the more challenging questions for adult social care, for example recovery in mental health and re-ablement for some people. We want to work with all of our stakeholders to develop a shared understanding of effectiveness and how this can be assessed.

Is this service caring?

❖ This could include the importance of staff being kind, empowering and treating people with dignity, respect and compassion, and how carers and family members are treated regulation and inspection of adult social care

Is this service responsive to people's needs?

❖ In social care, as well as meeting people's needs this is also about responding to people's preferences, aspirations and choices. We will want to know if care is personalised and puts the person at the centre in identifying their needs, choices and supporting them in the way they want to live their life. How the service responds to the needs of people living with more than one condition with complex care arrangements will be key, as will how the service recognises and understands the needs of people who lack capacity and responds to them appropriately.

Is this service well-led?

- ❖ In adult social care, this may look different depending on the size of the provider, but we know leadership is a key factor whatever the size of the service. We will also want to focus on the registered manager, as we know that the way they carry out their role has an important impact on setting the right culture, approach and leading good practice by example.

6Cs Care Values

The essential standards of quality and safety are described in CQC Guidance about compliance: Essential standards of quality and safety. They consist of a significant number of the Health and Social Care Act 2008 (Regulated Activities) Regulations 2010 and the Care Quality Commission (Registration) Regulations 2009. These regulations describe the essential standards of quality and safety that people who use health and adult social care services have a right to expect. A full list of the standards can be found within the Guidance about compliance.

Good practice in healthcare sector begins with the compliance of the rules and regulations, including code of conduct. The intentions of these frameworks are to set the minimum standards of behaviour and to maintain quality of service by implementing all the requirements. In response to Sir Francis Report on Mid-Staffordshire Hospital, the government in 2013 introduced "Recruitment 6Cs Values" as part of the effort to maintain skills and competences in healthcare sector. The 6Cs Values stands for:

- ➢ communication
- ➢ caring
- ➢ compassion

> ➢ competence
> ➢ commitment
> ➢ courage

These values are the behaviour attributes of a good healthcare worker. The government also introduced the fit and proper person requirements for director, and duty of candour.

To care is to empathise with your service
users and to understand their needs

The Fundamental Standards of Care

To allow easy compliance, the sixteen (16) essential standards (outcomes) of quality and safety were reduced to eleven (11) fundamental standards, plus the two additional regulations: fit and proper person requirements for directors of companies whose organisations provide care services, and duty of candour to ensure openness and trust. To ensure good practice, care workers should focus on understanding and practising the essential standards as below:

CARE QUALITY COMMISSION – THE FUNDAMENTAL STANDS OF CARE (01 APRIL 2015)

Regulation 4	Registration with CQC (Provider is individual/partnership)
Regulation 5	Fit and Proper Person – Directors
Regulation 6	Nominated Individual (supervising management of the regulated activities where the organisation is a body)
Regulation 7	Registered Manager (manage regulated activities provided)
Regulation 8	Registered Persons (must comply with the regulations)
Regulation 9	Person-Centred Care
Regulation 10	Dignity and Respect
Regulation 11	Need for Consent
Regulation 12	Safe Care and Treatment

Regulation 13	Safeguarding Services Users from Abuse and Improper Treatment
Regulation 14	Meeting Nutritional and Hydration Needs
Regulation 15	Cleanliness, Premises and Equipment
Regulation 16	Receiving and Acting on Complaints
Regulation 17	Good Governance
Regulation 18	Staffing
Regulation 19	Fit and Proper Person – Employed
Regulation 20	Duty of Candour (open and transparent)
Regulation 20A	Display of Assessment Rating (Conspicuous Areas)

Health and Social Care Act 2008 (Regulated Activities) Regulations 14

Care Quality Commission: Fundamental Standards Explained

Person-centred Care (Regulation 9)

> ➢ Person-centred care is the pivot on which the wheel of care rotates. All care plan must be centred around the patient's needs, and the patient or and his advocate must be involved in the care plan. Care plan must be carried out collaboratively with the service user. Any course of treatment must meet the need of the service user, and must be discussed with a relevant healthcare professional so as to inform the service user to understand all the benefits and effects of the treatment he or she is receiving, and to give consent to it. In this case, healthcare providers must communicate effectively for the understanding of the service user, to be fully informed of any care or treatment to be given to him, and for him to participate actively in the decision process.

Dignity and Respect (Regulation 10)

> ➢ Dignity and respect of the patient in your care must be maintained. All patients' dignity must be

preserved irrespective of any disability. In providing care, patient's rights must be respected. Supporting the autonomy, independence and involvement in the community of the service use. Having regards to the characteristics of the service user as contained in Equality Act 2010 and Gender Equality, and Human Rights Act 1998.

Need for Consent (Regulation 11)

> Need for consent is important. Patients' must be informed of any action to be taken on their behalf, and they, in the case of incapacity, with their advocate or legal representative must give their consent prior to any action being taken on their behalf, either to give care or treatment. This regulation is very important as it makes it clear that unsafe care and treated as a result of the consent of the service user must not be tolerated. Service provider must not give care and treatment that is unsafe just for obtaining consent of the service user. The safety of the service user must not be compromised. In this case, the service providers must use his professional judgement and duty of care in the provision of any care or treatment of

which the service user has given consent to, and this include managing medication and nutrition.

Safe Care and Treatment (Regulation 12)

> ➢ Safe care and treatment must be administered to patients. At NO time should unsafe care and treatment be given to a care user. Where this has happened, the patient must be notified immediately and adequate remedy must be administered to counter the negative effects. Risk assessment must be carried out by staff who have the qualifications, skills, competence and experience of the care and treatment which they offer to service users. In the case of equipment and medications, a reasonable quantity must be provided. Assessments of premises and equipment must be carried out regularly to maintain safe environment.

Safeguarding Service Users from Abuse (Regulation 13)

> ➢ Safeguarding service users from abuse is the responsibility of all care workers. It is advisable for care providers to watch the BBC 2014 panorama (elderly care exposed) as an eye opener. Such action is viewed as an abuse to the elderly and of course

any disabled person. Inhumane treatment is also considered as abuse, and any treatment of that nature is liable for prosecution. Care workers have duty of care for their patients and must safeguard them from any abuse. This regulation prohibits inappropriate and unlawful treatment and care such as discrimination, restraints and deprivation of liberty under Mental Health Act 2005. Abuse may be physical or mental and it also includes neglect, subjecting service user to a degrading and improper treatment. Any of these treatments must be avoided at all times.

Meeting Nutritional Needs (Regulation 14)

> ➤ Nutritional needs of a patient must be met. The management of nutrition and hydration must be adequate for a patient's needs, and in compliance with their religious and cultural values and beliefs. Care providers must ensure that adequate nutritious food and drinks according to the patient's need are provided to ensure a balanced diet and to sustain the life and good health of a patient. Anything short of this is a deliberate starvation and dehydration.

Premises and Equipment (Regulation 15)

> Cleanliness, safety and suitability of premises and equipment used for care provision must comply with the health and safety regulation at work. The premises and equipment must be secured, maintained and suitably located. The implication of this regulation is far reaching. The premises and equipment must be fit for purpose, and must be cleaned, maintained standards of hygiene to ensure their suitability for the use of service users. Equipment must be properly secured and properly used.

Receiving and acting on complaints (Regulation 16)

> There must be a system of identifying, receiving, recording, handling and responding to complaints made by service users and others in relation to the services provided. Complaints must be appropriately investigated and appropriate response given to the complainant. Any complaints made by your clients, or his or her representative, must follow the appropriate procedures to investigate the issue without bias and prejudice, to the satisfaction of the

client. The outcomes of the investigation must be appropriately communicated to the complainant.

Good Governance (Regulation 17)

> ➢ Systems and processes must be established to ensure compliance of the fundamental standards. The management must provide appropriate policies and procedures that meet the required standards. The healthcare worker is duty bound to follow the procedures as stipulated by the management, unless where it is observed that it does not meet its requirements. In that case, such observation must be brought to the attention of the management. In many cases, it is the frontline staff who are in a better position to understand if a procedure is effective or not.

Staffing (regulation 18)

> ➢ This regulation made it clear that sufficient number of suitably qualified, skilful and experienced staff must be employed to carry out work in healthcare sector. This enabled the government in 2013, in response to Sir Francis Report on Mid-Staffordshire Hospital Trust, introduced recruitment 6Cs. This provision

advised employers to look out for these qualities when recruiting workers in healthcare sector. It also advises employers to train the already recruited workforce to acquire these qualities. In order for any healthcare worker to be successful and competent, he or she must endeavour to seek and acquire these relevant skills. These qualities may be part of selection processes, either through aptitude test or psychometric test, and if missed during the shortlisting process, it may form part of the topics to be explored at face-to-face interviews. The management must have a system of support, training, professional development, supervision and assessment to make sure that staff are competent enough to carry out the tasks of which they are employed.

Fit and Proper Persons Employed (Regulation 19)

> ➤ The person employed must be of good character, have relevant qualifications, be competent, skilful and experience to perform the tasks of which they employed. There must be a system of appraisal that assesses their suitability. The person employed must be of sound health, and mentally alert to make judgement in the case of ethical dilemma. This regulation allows employers to have appropriate

system of recruitment in place so as to employ healthcare workers who are competent. The system will include the use of DBS (Disclosure and Barring Services), monitoring performance of employee for suitability, continuous assessment for professional development, and appropriate supervision by provision a mentor.

Duty of Candour (Regulation 20)

➤ This regulation mandates healthcare providers to be open and transparent with their service users of any incidents that may occur in their care and treatment. The openness and transparency is to inform service users and their representatives of any incidents, no matter how small it may be, the true nature of the incidents, the outcomes of such incidents to their care and treatment. The service provider must inform service users of any further enquiries relating to the incidents, and to offer unreserved apology. The service provider must offer adequate support, record the incident in the incident book according and this information must be secured. Healthcare worker must note that the true account of the incident must be provided to the service user and their authorised representative.

Organisations and Managers Only

Fit and Proper Person for Directors (regulation 5)

> This regulation made it clear that any person with the responsibility of a director in healthcare provision must be fit and proper. This means that he or she must be of good character, and has not committed or privy to committing any offence that may render him unfit. The director or person with the responsibility of a director must have relevant qualifications, skills, competence and experience relevant to the level of work that he or she does. The director or person acting on that level must be of good health and mentally sound for the performance of his or her task in managing healthcare provision to service users.

Display of Performance Assessment (Regulation 20A)

> This fundamental standard mandates healthcare providers to display rating of their most recent performance assessment by care quality commission (CQC). This is in continuation of the duty of candour as it works to promote openness and transparency. The Rating display must be at a conspicuous place at any of their place or work. The display of rating includes websites and wherever organisations display their business for either marketing or provision of their services.

Be transparent

HealthCare Organisations and Their Legal Duties

In addition to Health and Social Care Act 2008 (Regulated Activities) Regulations 2014, there is also Care Act 2014 that focuses on the wellbeing of care users. For organisations offering services in healthcare sector to satisfy their customers (patients or care users), there are legislations, regulations (statutory instruments) and policies designed to guide practices and compliance at workplace. Under the Health and Safety at Work Act 1974, and Management of health and Safety at Work (MHSW) Regulations 1999, employers have legal duties to maintain care safety standard in the United Kingdom.

The following guide daily routines at healthcare workplace, and the implementations of patients' safety and wellbeing:

- ❖ Health and Social Care Act 2008 (Regulated Activities) Regulations 2014
- ❖ Care Act 2014
- ❖ Health and Safety at Work Act 1974
- ❖ Management of Health and Safety at Work Regulations 1999
- ❖ Safety Representatives and Safety Committees Regulations 1997

- ❖ Data Protection Act 1998
- ❖ Equality Act 2010
- ❖ Human Rights Act 1998
- ❖ Safeguarding Vulnerable Group Act 2006
- ❖ Health and Safety (Fire Aid) Regulations 1981
- ❖ International Development (Gender Equality) Act 2014
- ❖ Freedom of Information Act 2005
- ❖ Care Quality Commission (Registration) Regulations 2009
- ❖ Control of Substances Hazardous to Health (COSHH) Regulations 2002
- ❖ Reporting of Injuries, Diseases and Dangerous Occurrences Regulations (RIDDOR) 1995
- ❖ Disclosure of Barring Services (DBS) established by Police Act 1997 (Criminal Records) (Registration) Regulations 2006
- ❖ Provision and Use of Work Equipment Regulations (PUWER) 1998
- ❖ The Work Place (Health, Safety and Welfare) Regulations 1992
- ❖ Manual Handling Operations Regulations 1992
- ❖ Lifting Operations and Lifting Equipment Regulations (LOLER) 1998
- ❖ The Regulatory Reform (Fire Safety) Order (RRO) 2005

* ❖ Confidentiality: NHS Code of Practice 2003
* ❖ NHS England: Confidentiality Policy, June 2014
* ❖ NICE Managing Medicine In Care Home Policy March 2014
* ❖ Personal Protective Equipment at Work (PPE) Regulations 1992

Organisational Systems and Procedures for Compliance of the Law

Organisations in health and social care sector must adhere to the above legislations and regulations. The organisational policies and procedures must be designed to comply with the provisions of the above legislations and regulations. It is duty bound for the management of any organisation to draw up policies and procedures to implement national policies. Most of these legislations and regulations concerning healthcare industry is monitored and enforces by Care Quality Commission for England and Local Authorities. The Health and Social Care Act 2008, part 1, chapter 1, section 1, paragraph 1 and 2 set out the Care Quality Commission (CQC) to be the regulating body for health and social care. This legislation set out the Commission and empowered the Secretary of State to dissolve the commission for healthcare audit and inspection, the commission for social care inspection, and the mental health act commission. To make sure that good practice is maintained in health and social care, chapter 2, article 8, paragraph 1 and 2 set out the regulated activities. The Act, chapter 3, article 45, paragraphs 1, 2 and 3 set out the health care standards. Care Quality Commission is established, given the power to set out and review care quality standards with consultation with the public and healthcare users. This body is given the power to regulation the industry and to enforce the compliance to ensure quality standards.

Understand the rules and remove
the barriers to quality service

Healthcare Organisations and workers must comply with the law

CQC Fundamental Standards, Part 4

Evidence Gathering

"The CQC says that their intelligence gathering system is called Intelligent Monitoring, and it is used to identify when where and what to inspect. This approach is key to their policy of targeting scarce inspection resource where it is most needed."

The Key Lines of Enquiry (KLOEs)

KLOE

- Safe
- Effective
- Caring
- Responsive
- Well-led

Quality Compliance System

CQC collaborate and shares information with Local Authority Healthwatch "Enter and View" Report on:

- Notification
- Safeguarding alerts
- Reports from users of services
- Report from the staff
- Report from the public

The CQC Schematic for Registration and Inspection

- ➢ Registration
- ➢ Intelligent monitoring
- ➢ Expert inspections
- ➢ Judgement and publication
- ➢ Action

The Fundamental Standards Part 5, Inspection

Some key overall points are:

Community services inspections will usually be pre-announced 48 hours before they will take place. This is not done in order to negotiate a suitable day, but to inform the service that the inspection is to take place on the appointed day, and to make sure that the manager, or a senior person in charge, is there on the day. "A senior person in charge" implies a working deputy to the manager if the manager is unavoidably absent. This is not the Provider if they are not in day-to-day management control, and therefore not able to provide detailed operational information. The inspector is interested in what is actually happening in the service, not what the Provider hopes or assumes is happening.

For Residential Services: Site Inspection Is Unannounced

CQC Inspection Is Dependent on Rating

- ✓ Inadequate - within 6 months of the last inspection
- ✓ Requires Improvement - within 12 months of the last inspection
- ✓ Good - within 18 months of the last inspection
- ✓ Outstanding - within 24 months of the last inspection

THE INSPECTION IS BASED ON SERVICE USER'S FEELING AND UNDERSTANDING OF YOUR PERFORMANCE AND IMPROVEMENT THAT IS GATHERED THROUGH QUESTIONNAIRE-BASED SURVEY

Planning for Inspection	The Site Visit	Closing the Visit
The CQC inspection planning will take into account: ➢ Intelligent monitoring, as explained in our previous article ➢ Registration information ➢ Previous inspection reports and follow-ups ➢ Comments and feedback from people who use the service, and the public ➢ Healthwatch feedback ➢ Local voluntary and community groups, including equality groups ➢ Feedback from questionnaires sent by the CQC ➢ Feedback from telephone interviews	The inspector will inform you which Key Lines of Enquiry they will be inspecting, and: • Whether they are following up on any previous issues • The proposed length of the inspection • The roles of the inspection team members • Who they plan to speak with • Documents they want to review • How they will feedback about what was found during the inspection	At this meeting the inspector will: • Explain what has been found during the visit • Highlight any issues that have emerged • Explain that this is preliminary feedback and that they cannot make a judgement until they have considered all the evidence together. For example, there may be evidence from Experts by Experience to analyse, or feedback from people they could not speak with on the day

➤ Information from other agencies. Fire and environmental agencies are mentioned for residential services, but none are specified for community services. ➤ The Provider Information Return (see a later article) ➤ Statutory notifications ➤ Applications for variation of registration ➤ Information from staff, in the form of feedback from questionnaires		• Say when the report can be expected, how any factual inaccuracies can be challenged and what the publishing arrangements are • Answer any questions from the person in charge and receive their feedback on the inspection process so far • Say what the next steps will be

Local Policies and Procedures for Good Practice

Confidentiality

It is provided under Data Protection Act 1998 to protect the collection, storing, distribution, use, processing, disclosure and destroying of personal and organisational information. Personal information includes the name, the date of birth, and the address of a person. This also include the profession, the age, personal attribute and any other information that may, under careful examination, may reveal the identity of a person. Handling of the information must be confidential, and can only be disclosed by the request of a court or police in pursuit of crime and for the protection of the public.

A lot has been made by the handling of confidentiality and has sometimes, led to confusion. In health and social care, there are policies relating to confidentiality: NHS Code of Practice, November 2003; NHS England Confidentiality

Policy June 2014. To avoid further confusion, the Secretary of State, under the Health and Social Care Act 2012, part 9, chapter 2, article 252, paragraph 2, established Health and Social Care Information Centre as a body to streamline the use of confidential information in England and Wales. This body is responsible for reviewing policies on patient confidentiality, and to advise organisations on how to handle it for compliance of the law and for the satisfaction of their service users. It is good and advisable for organisations to draw their confidentiality policy based on Caldicott Rules.

Caldicott Seven (7) Principles (To Share or Not to Share) September 2013

Dame Fiona Caldicott, Chair of Information Governance Review, and Kingsley Manning, Chair of Health and Social Care Information Centre, published "A Guide to Confidentiality in Health and Social Care in September 2013, and identified seven principles on protection and sharing of confidential information:

> ➢ Justify the purpose(s)
> ➢ Do not use personal confidential data unless it is absolutely necessary
> ➢ Use the minimum necessary personal confidential data
> ➢ Access to personal confidential data should be on a strict need-to-know basis
> ➢ Everyone with access to personal confidential data should be aware of their responsibilities
> ➢ Comply with the law
> ➢ The duty to share information can be as important as the duty to protect confidential information

It is noteworthy that the Caldicott principles 2013 of sharing personal confidential data allows health and social care professionals to be confident in sharing information in the best interests of their patients.

HSCIC 2013: The Five (5) Rules of Confidentiality Disclosure

The Health and Social Care Information Centre (HSCIC) was empowered as a body to provide advice and guidance on the matters relating to the collection, analysis, publication and other dissemination of information. After due consultations, it published five rules as code of practice for collecting, processing and sharing of confidential information of their clients for their best interest and the interest of the community.

These rules are:

Rule 1	Confidential information about service users or patients should be treated confidentially and respectfully
Rule 2	Members of a care team should share confidential information when it is needed for the safe and effective care of an individual
Rule 3	Information that is shared for the benefits of the community should be anonymised
Rule 4	An individual's right to object to the sharing of confidential information about them should be respected
Rule 5	Organisations should put policies, procedures and systems in place to ensure the confidentiality rules are followed.

Health and Safety at Work 1974 and the Management of Health and Safety at Work Regulations 1999

It is mandatory for organisations to comply with the rules and regulations guiding Health and Safety at Work (HASAW) Act 1974. Employers and employees have responsibilities to ensure that they adhere to the rules and regulations guiding safety at work, and their actions would not put the life and safety of any one at risk. The Management of Health and Safety at Work regulations 1999 mandates employers to assess risks, keep records if employed five people or more, identify preventive and protective measures To design, review and update policies in compliance with the Act. It also requires employer to appoint a health and safety representative, who will be a contact person, responsible for managing health and safety issues, although the directors and in most cases, senior managers of a company are collectively responsible to comply with the rules and regulations. In compliance, health and social care workers and their managers are collectively responsible for safety and welfare of their care users or patients and others within their premises. There are five steps to follow when carrying out risk assessment at workplace, names:

> ➤ Identify potential Hazards
> ➤ Identify who might be harmed and how

> ➢ Evaluate the risks and decide on precautions
> ➢ Record your findings and implement them
> ➢ Review your risk assessment and update them if necessary

Healthcare providers should also know that it is mandatory to consult employees and the union regarding the safety of their employees and other workers. The Safety Representatives and Safety Committees Regulations 1997 (Safety representatives and Safety Committees Regulations 1977 and 1996 (as amended) stipulates that Safety Representatives and Safety Committees should be appointed, staff and representatives to be consulted in risk assessment affecting the workforce. All arrangements and changes concerning the safety of the workforce should be communicated to the representatives and to get them involved in the assessment of risks that may affect the workers.

Application of COSHH Regulations 2002

The application of COSHH Regulations 2002 is a daily routine for a health and social care workers. The employer must design policy, procedures and systems to implement the management of substances such as washing up liquid, washing powders, bleach and others that may harm their patients. All these must be locked away and there must be record of who uses them. The recording may discourage carelessness and misuse by any worker. It is advisable for any health and social care worker to follow the procedures stipulated by their management. Health workers must endeavour to read and understand the procedures though, it is mandatory for the employer to provide adequate training on how to comply with the application of COSHH.

Keep away all liquids

Application of RIDDOR 1995

RIDDOR (Recording of Incidents, Diseases and Dangerous Occurrences Regulations) 1995 and as amended 2013

Under Health and Safety at Work Act 1974: reporting of incidents, diseases and dangerous occurrences regulations 1995 and as amended 2013, there must be recording and record keeping of any incidents that occurred within the premises or outside if a service user is involved. Incidents could be anything that is life threatening, injury or any injury causing incidents that may have caused injuries should it have happened, death and emotional trauma to a service user, staff or any other persons within the premises. The regulation required that diseases or any contagious illness that may be directly or indirectly transmitted to other people must be reported, recorded and kept secured. The responsible person must notify care quality commission accordingly.

The regulation requires that an employer must have in place policies and procedures to implement the requirements. A health and social worker must endeavour to record accordingly as the organisational policy and procedures stipulate. The health and social care workers must endeavour to read, understand and acquaint themselves of the skills to comply with RIDDOR policy and procedures though, it is mandatory for employer to provide training to educate workers on how to understand and implement any aspects of health and safety at work. As a health and social worker, your manager, supervisor or mentor must guide you in the right direction regarding the compliance with any health and safety issue. None compliance with health and safety issues may result to prosecution, imprisonment, fine, compensation or blacklisting within health and social care sector.

Equality Act 2010 and Human Rights Act 1998

Equality and Human Rights Commission (EHRC) is responsible for the protection and promotion of equality and human rights in the United Kingdom. According to the Government Equality Office, the Minister for Women and Equalities, Mrs Nicky Morgan (MP) press release 23 January 2015 stated that the Equality and Human Rights Commission is a statutory body established under the Equality Act 2006. EHRC is an independent body responsible for protecting and promoting equality and human rights in Great Britain. It aims to encourage equality and diversity, eliminate unlawful discrimination, and promote and protect human rights. The commission enforces equality legislation on age, disability, gender reassignment, marriage and civil partnership, pregnancy and maternity, race, religion or belief, sex, sexual orientation. It encourages compliance with the Human Rights Act 1998 and is accredited by the UN as an 'A status' national human rights institution.

The above legislations require an employer to have in place of work policy, procedures and systems to ensure compliance. The policy must direct employees of how to implement equality and human rights in health and social care sector. This is important to ensure that no patients or care users may be discriminated upon, irrespective of the religious and cultural beliefs of the health and social workers employed in that organisation. A breach of these legislations may result to prosecution. The onus is on the employee to acquaint themselves with the policy and procedures of compliance though the law requires the employer to provide adequate training to enable the employee to acquire skills to enable the implementation.

The Care Act 2014: Safeguarding Vulnerable Group (Adults at risk)

It is important for any health and social care worker or service provider to be aware of safeguarding vulnerable adults, children and young people. The rules and regulations made it clear that it is an offence to carry out any form of abuse to vulnerable people. To understand the implications, the Office of the Public Guardian's policy stated that Safeguarding relates to the need to protect certain people who may be in vulnerable circumstances. These are people who may be at risk of abuse or neglect, due to the actions (or lack of action) of another person. It continues that in these cases, it is critical that services work together to identify people at risk, and put in place interventions to help prevent abuse or neglect, and to protect people.

According to the Office of the Public Guardian (OPG): Safeguarding Policy, May 2013, abuse is a violation of an individual's human and civil rights by another person or persons. Abuse may consist of a single act or repeated acts. It may be physical, financial, verbal or psychological or an act of neglect or omission to act. It may occur when an adult at risk is persuaded to enter into a financial or sexual transaction to which s/he has not consented, or cannot consent. Abuse can occur in any relationship and may result in significant harm to, or exploitation of, the person subjected to it. The categories of abuse as defined by the Office of the Public Guardian are identified below:

Safeguarding Adults at Risk Legislations

- ➢ Care Act 2014
- ➢ Protection of Freedom Act 2012
- ➢ Freedom of Information Act 2004
- ➢ Safeguarding Vulnerable Groups Act 2006
- ➢ Mental Capacity Act 2005
- ➢ Equality Act 2010
- ➢ Data Protection Act 1998

Types of Abuse

1. Physical Abuse
2. Sexual Abuse
3. Emotional or Psychological Abuse
4. Financial or Material abuse
5. Discrimination Abuse
6. Organisational abuse
7. Domestic Violence
8. Neglect or act of omission
9. Modern Slavery
10. Self-Neglect
11. Use of Social media in an abusive way

Physical Abuse	Physical abuse includes hitting, slapping, pushing, kicking, and misuse of medication, restraint or inappropriate sanctions.
Financial abuse	Financial abuse can range from failure to access benefits, through inadvertent mismanagement and opportunistic exploitation to deliberate and targeted abuse, often accompanied by threats and intimidation. It can include theft, fraud, exploitation, pressure in connection with wills, property or inheritance or financial transactions, overcharging or carrying out unnecessary work, or the misuse or misappropriation of property, possessions or benefits
Sexual abuse	Includes rape and sexual assault or sexual acts to which the adult at risk has not consented, or could not consent or was pressured into consenting.
Psychological or emotional abuse	Includes emotional abuse, threats of harm or abandonment, deprivation of contact, humiliation, blaming, controlling, intimidation, coercion, harassment, verbal abuse, isolation or withdrawal from services or supporting networks

Neglect and acts of omission	Includes ignoring medical or physical care needs, failure to provide access to appropriate health, social care or educational services, the withholding of the necessities of life, such as medication, adequate nutrition and heating. Research has shown that neglect is the most prevalent form of abuse of elders in the UK, with financial abuse a close second
Discriminatory abuse	Includes ageist, racist, sexist, that based on a persons disability, and other forms of harassment, slurs or similar treatment
Institutional abuse	The mistreatment or abuse or neglect of an adult at risk by a regime or individuals within settings and services that adults at risk live in or use, that violate the person's dignity, resulting in lack of respect for their human rights. Institutional abuse occurs when the routines, systems and regimes of an institution result in poor or inadequate standards of care and poor practice which affects the whole setting and denies restricts or curtails the dignity, privacy, choice, independence or fulfilment of adults at risk.

Abuse of trust	A relationship of trust is one in which one person is in a position of power or influence over the other person because of their work or the nature of their activity. There is a particular concern when abuse is caused by the actions or omissions of someone who is in a position of power or authority and who uses their position to the detriment of the health and well-being of a person at risk, who in many cases could be dependent on their care. There is always a power imbalance in a relationship of trust.
Mate crime	Mate crime is a type of hate crime where perpetrators befriend a person with a disability but in fact soon begin to exploit, hurt or harm them. This can include sexual abuse, forced prostitution, financial exploitation, physical abuse, violence and even murder
Domestic violence	Including psychological, physical, sexual, financial, emotional abuse; so called 'honour' based violence. And can affect those it is not aimed at within the home.

Neglect and acts of omission	Including ignoring medical or physical care needs, failure to provide access to appropriate health, social care and support or educational services or equipment for functional independence, the withholding of the necessities of life, such as medication, adequate nutrition, heating and lighting. Failure to give privacy and dignity.
Modern slavery	Encompasses slavery, human trafficking, forced labour and domestic servitude. Traffickers and slave masters use whatever means they have at their disposal to coerce, deceive and force individuals into a life of abuse, servitude and inhumane treatment.
Discriminatory abuse	Including forms of harassment, slurs or similar treatment; because of race, colour, language, gender and gender identity, age, disability, sexual orientation or religion. Hate crime

Organisational abuse	Including neglect and poor care practice within an institution or specific care setting such as a hospital or care home, for example, or in relation to care provided in one's own home. This may range from one off incidents to on-going ill-treatment. It can be through neglect or poor professional practice as a result of the structure, policies, processes and practices within an organisation
Self-Neglect	This covers a wide range of behaviour, neglecting to care for one's personal hygiene, health or surroundings and includes behaviour such as hoarding. Safeguarding within the Affiliated Group
Use of Social Media in an abusive way	Abuse can also occur through social media and this is often harder to detect. It is important to remember that the type of abuse that can occur through social media does not always include emotional and psychological abuse and can include sexual and financial abuse. Social media includes (but is not limited to): networking sites such as Facebook, Twitter and LinkedIn, email, text messages, Skype and instant messaging services

Read Easy: Adult Safeguarding Policy 2018

The Office of the Public Guardian (OPG) stated that abuse can take many forms. It does not have to fit comfortably into any of the above. Abuse can be perpetuated by one adult at risk towards another. This is still abuse and should be dealt with accordingly. The adult at risk may also be neglecting him/herself which could also justify a safeguarding referral.

Mental Capacity Act (MCA) 2005

Organisations and service providers must put in place policy, procedures and systems to ensure that they comply with safeguarding vulnerable people. They must also provide training for the workers to acquire the skills and experience of keeping their service users protected from harm and abuse. Any workers abusing vulnerable people are liable for prosecution. There is now a zero tolerance and any forms of abuse are prohibited. Health and social care workers must be aware that nothing is hidden under the sun, and any form of abuse will at some point be identified and punished accordingly. The onus is upon you as a health and social worker to make sure that you acquaint yourself with the policy, procedures and system to protect vulnerable people.

For more information, please refer to the OPG's Safeguarding policy, May 2013. The Office of the Public Guardian is sponsored by the Ministry of Justice and established by Mental Capacity Act (MCA) 2005, to protect people at risk of abuse or neglect.

Legislations Guiding Safeguarding Vulnerable Group

- ➢ Safeguarding Vulnerable Groups Act 2006
- ➢ Data Protection Act 1998
- ➢ The Human Rights Act 1998
- ➢ Police Reform Act 2002
- ➢ Health and Social Care Act 2008 (Regulated Activities) Regulations 2014 (Human Rights Act 1998
- ➢ Equality Act 2010
- ➢ Mental Capacity Act 2005
- ➢ Person-Centred Care (Regulation 9)
- ➢ Dignity and Respect (Regulation 10)
- ➢ Need for Consent (Regulation 11)
- ➢ Safe Care and Treatment (Regulation 12)
- ➢ Safeguarding Service Users (Regulation 13) regulation13)

Safeguarding Policies

- ❖ The Charities Act 2006
- ❖ The Protection of Freedoms Act 2012 (DBS)
- ❖ Charities Commission May 2013
- ❖ Sir Michael Bichard Report 2004
- ❖ Fraser Guidelines (House of Lords 1985)
- ❖ Gillick Competency Assessment (Lord Scarman 1985)
- ❖ SOVA (Safeguarding of Vulnerable Adult)
- ❖ Safeguarding Children and Young People (Under 18yrs) Policy Paper 14th July 2014
- ❖ Disclosure of Barring Services (DBS)
- ❖ Deprivation of Liberty (DoL)

Professionals Working For Achievement of Safeguarding

- ✓ Independent Safeguarding Authority (ISA)
- ✓ Local Authorities (Social Services)
- ✓ Charities Commission
- ✓ Police (ACPO/HMIC)
- ✓ Health and Social Care professionals
- ✓ Care Quality Commission (CQC)
- ✓ Office of the Public Guardian (OPG)
- ✓ NSPCC
- ✓ NHS England
- ✓ Department of Health

Safeguarding Inter-Agency Working

- ➢ Charity Commission
- ➢ NSPCC
- ➢ Save the Children
- ➢ Christian Aid
- ➢ People in Aid
- ➢ EveryChild
- ➢ Tearfund
- ➢ NCVYS

National Framework Standards and Safeguarding

- ➤ Standard 2: Partners recognise/accountable Safeguarding
- ➤ Standard 3: SA Policy to include rights to live free of abuse
- ➤ Standard 4: Policy on Zero-Tolerance of Abuse and Neglect
- ➤ Standard 5: Ensure appropriate development/training
- ➤ Standard 6: Access to info on safety from abuse/violence
- ➤ Standard 7: Local Multi-Agency policies and procedures
- ➤ Standard 8: Partners have policy/procedures in line with LP
- ➤ Standard 9: Multi-Agency has detailed procedures of stages
- ➤ Standard 10: Safeguarding procedures be accessible to all
- ➤ Standard 11: Include service users as partners at all stages

Personal Protective Equipment at Work (PPE) Regulations 1992

The Personal protective Equipment at Work Regulations 1992 is a requirement under the Health and Safety at Work Act 1974 for employers to provide protective equipment for their employees to protect them from harm. Health and Safety Executives (HSE) describe PPE as equipment that will protect the user against health or safety risks at work. It can include items such as safety helmets and hard hats, gloves, eye protection, high-visibility clothing, safety footwear and safety harnesses. Employer is required to provide the equipment free of charge. The free provision of PPE includes agency workers. There should be adequate training and instruction on the use of personal protective equipment. The regulations require an employer to consult the employees or their appointed representative when deciding to choose the correct equipment for use at workplace. To prevent harm, an employee or indeed any worker must comply with the use of PPE. Refusal to use the personal protective equipment as instructed by any worker is a breach of health and safety regulations. Below are how the Personal Protective Equipment at Work Regulations 1992 identified the risks and the need to use it so as to prevent harm.

The hazards and types of PPE (Regulations 1992)

Eyes	Hazards: Chemical or metal splash, dust, projectiles, gas and vapour, radiation. Options: Safety spectacles, goggles, face-shields, visors. Note: Make sure the eye protection has the right combination of impact/dust/splash/molten metal eye protection for the task and fits the user properly
Head	Hazards: Impact from falling or flying objects, risk of head bumping, hair entanglement. Options: A range of helmets, hard hats and bump caps. Note: Some safety helmets incorporate or can be fitted with specially-designed eye or hearing protection. Don't forget neck protection, eg scarves for use during welding. Do not use head protection if it is damaged – replace it.
Breathing	Hazards: Dust, vapour, gas, oxygen-deficient atmospheres. Options: Disposable filtering face-piece or respirator, half- or full-face respirators, airfed helmets, breathing apparatus. Note: The right type of respirator filter must be used as each is effective for only a limited range of substances. Where there is a shortage of oxygen or any danger of losing consciousness due to exposure to high levels of harmful fumes, only use breathing apparatus – never use a filtering cartridge. Filters only have a limited life; when replacing them or any other part, check with the manufacturer's guidance and ensure the correct replacement part is used. If you are using respiratory protective equipment, look at HSE's publication Respiratory protective equipment at work: A practical guide (see 'Further reading')

Protecting the body	Hazards: Temperature extremes, adverse weather, chemical or metal splash, spray from pressure leaks or spray guns, impact or penetration, contaminated dust, excessive wear or entanglement of own clothing. Options: Conventional or disposable overalls, boiler suits, specialist protective clothing, eg chain-mail aprons, high-visibility clothing. Note: The choice of materials includes flame-retardant, anti-static, chain mail, chemically impermeable, and high-visibility. Also included are safety harnesses and lifejackets
Hands and arms	Hazards: abrasion, temperature extremes, cuts and punctures, impact, chemicals, electric shock, skin infection, disease or contamination. Options: Gloves, gauntlets, mitts, wrist-cuffs, armlets. Note: Avoid gloves when operating machines such as bench drills where the gloves could get caught. Some materials are quickly penetrated by chemicals so be careful when you are selecting them, see HSE's skin at work website (www.hse.gov.uk/skin)
Feet and legs	*Hazards: Wet, electrostatic build-up, slipping, cuts and punctures, falling objects, metal and chemical splash, abrasion. Options: Safety boots and shoes with protective toe caps and penetration-resistant mid-sole, gaiters, leggings, spats. Note: Footwear can have a variety of sole patterns and materials to help prevent slips in different conditions, including oil or chemical-resistant soles. It can also be anti-static, electrically conductive or thermally insulating. It is important that the appropriate footwear is selected for the risks identified*

The Manual Handling Operations Regulations 1992

Manual Handling is very important in health and social care sector. This is a provision of Health and Safety at Work Act 1974. It is mandatory for employers to assess the risks involved in lifting, such as patients, beddings, equipment and others. The rule demands that there must be a policy, system and procedures for lifting at workplace. It is also mandatory for employees and other workforce to adhere to it as it is an offence to intentionally ignore the procedures. The employer must provide adequate training and instructions on how to manage and comply with the policy of lifting at work. The Manual Handling Operations Regulations 1992 prescribes below, the basic methods on how the employer and employee can comply with the regulations:

The Duties of employers state that each employer shall:

So far as is reasonably practicable, avoid the need for his employees to undertake any manual handling operations at work which involve a risk of their being injured. Where it is not reasonably practicable to avoid the need for his employees to undertake any manual handling operations at work which involve a risk of their being injured:—

    (i) Make a suitable and sufficient assessment of all such manual handling operations to be undertaken by them, having regard to the factors which are specified in column 1 of Schedule 1 to these Regulations and considering the questions which are specified in the corresponding entry in column 2 of that Schedule.

    (ii) Take appropriate steps to reduce the risk of injury to those employees arising out of their undertaking any such manual handling operations to the lowest level reasonably practicable.

    (iii) Take appropriate steps to provide any of those employees who are undertaking any such manual handling operations with general indications and, where it is reasonably practicable to do so, precise information on—

(a) The weight of each load, and

(b) The heaviest side of any load whose centre of gravity is not positioned centrally.

Doing tasks involve the following:-

> ➤ Holding or manipulating loads at distance from trunk?
> ➤ Unsatisfactory bodily movement or posture, especially:
> ➤ Twisting the trunk?
> ➤ Stooping?
> ➤ Reaching upwards?
> ➤ Excessive movement of loads, especially:
> ➤ Excessive lifting or lowering distances?
> ➤ Excessive carrying distances?
> ➤ Excessive pushing or pulling of loads?
> ➤ Risk of sudden movement of loads?
> ➤ Frequent or prolonged physical effort?
> ➤ Insufficient rest or recovery periods?
> ➤ A rate of work imposed by a process?

The regulations state that any assessment such as is referred to above shall be reviewed by the employer who made it if—

(a) There is reason to suspect that it is no longer valid; or
(b) There has been a significant change in the manual handling operations to which it relates; and where as a result of any such review changes to an assessment are required, the relevant employer shall make them.

The Duty of Employees

Each employee while at work shall make full and proper use of any system of work provided for his use by his employer in compliance with the regulations. The loads must be assessed to identify if they are:

> - Heavy?
> - Bulky or unwieldy?
> - Difficult to grasp?
> - Unstable, or with contents likely to shift?
> - Sharp, hot or otherwise potentially damaging?

The working environment must also be assessed to identify if any of the following apply:

> - Space constraints preventing good posture?
> - Uneven, slippery or unstable floors?
> - Variations in level of floors or work surfaces?
> - Extremes of temperature or humidity?
> - Conditions causing ventilation problems or gusts of wind?
> - Poor lighting conditions?

Individual capability for the job shall be assessed accordingly to identify if the following apply:

> ➤ Does the job require unusual strength, height, etc.?
> ➤ Does the job create a hazard to those who might reasonably be considered to be pregnant or to have a health problem?
> ➤ Does the job require special information or training for its safe performance?

HSE Advice for Workers and Employers

The Health and Safety Executives (HSE) provided explanations to the above regulations. It stated that there is need to comply with the risk assessment requirements set out in the Management of Health and Safety at Work Regulations 1999 as well as the requirement in the Manual Handling Operations Regulations 1992 (as amended) (MHOR) to carry out a risk assessment on manual handling tasks as stated above and below.

The MHOR Regulations 1992 in Brief

The employer's duty is to avoid Manual Handling as far as reasonably practicable if there is a possibility of injury. If this cannot be done then they must reduce the risk of injury as far as reasonably practicable. If an employee is complaining of discomfort, any changes to work to avoid or reduce manual handling must be monitored to check they are having a positive effect. However, if they are not working satisfactorily, alternatives must be considered.

The regulations set out a hierarchy of measures to reduce the risks of manual handling. These are in regulation 4(1) and as follows:

> ➢ Avoid hazardous manual handling operations so far as reasonably practicable
> ➢ Assess any hazardous manual handling operations that cannot be avoided
> ➢ Reduce the risk of injury so far as reasonably practicable.

The guidance on the Manual Handling Regulations includes a risk assessment filter and checklist to help employers assess manual handling tasks. A revised version of the MHOR was published in March 2004. It also includes a checklist to help you assess the risk(s) posed by workplace pushing and pulling activities.

In addition, employees have duties to take reasonable care of their own health and safety and that of others who may be affected by their actions. They must communicate with their employers so that they too are able to meet their health and safety duties.

Employees have general health and safety duties to:

> ➢ follow appropriate systems of work laid down for their safety
> ➢ make proper use of equipment provided for their safety
> ➢ co-operate with their employer on health and safety matters
> ➢ inform the employer if they identify hazardous handling activities
> ➢ take care to ensure that their activities do not put others at risk

In any care home or hospital, there is a range of equipment designed to ease patient handling. Being an employee or worker in healthcare sector, your employer must provide relevant patient handling equipment, train you on how to handle and operate them, provide you with adequate instruction on the usage, and it is your responsibility to make sure that you comply with the usage. The manual handling equipment in healthcare sector includes:

> ➢ Hoist
> ➢ Sliding seat
> ➢ Wheel chair

- ➢ Turntable
- ➢ Raiser seat
- ➢ Stairlift/elevator
- ➢ Shower trolleys
- ➢ Shower stretcher
- ➢ Patient sling
- ➢ Shower chair, etc.

Care Plan

First and foremost, a care plan is centred on the patient or service user. According to NHS Choice, a care plan is an agreement between patient and health professional (or social services) to help the service user to manage his or her health day to day. It can be a written document or something recorded in your patient notes. It continues that everyone who has a long-term condition can take part in making their care plan. It helps to assess what care you need and how it will be provided.

NHS Choice also recommends that a Care plan should include:

> ➢ The goals you (the patient or care user) want to work towards, such as getting out of the house more, returning to work, or starting a hobby.
> ➢ The support services you want, who is in charge of providing these services, what the support services have agreed to do, and when they will do it
> ➢ Emergency numbers, such as who you should contact if you become very unwell and your doctor's surgery is closed
> ➢ Medicines
> ➢ An eating plan
> ➢ An exercise plan

The Health and Social Care Act 2008 (Regulated Activities) Regulations 2014 demands that Person Centred Approach must be adopted when preparing a care plan. It demands that patient or service user must be consulted and given enough time for him and his advocate to prepare for any meeting relating to care plan. The patient or service user must be given the opportunity to contribute to the decision making and his or her choice must be respected. Care plan also require partnership with all the professionals who are involved for the welfare of the patient. These include GP, the physiologist, the nutritionist, the local authority, the police and of course, the service provider (carer or nurse). In doing this, the focus must be on the patient's wellbeing, so as to give him or her, the best possible care. When preparing a care plan, it is important to focus on what the patient or service user wants. This calls for working in partnership with other stakeholders and professionals for holistic care plan for a service user.

CARE PLAN LOG SHEET									
Name of Patient:______________________________									
Name of Organisation:__________________________									
Date									Total Time with Patient
Development of Care									
Care Plan Revision									
Patient's Report Review									
Laboratory Review									
Review of Diagnostic Test									
Communication with Professional Partners									
Integrating new Info into care plan									
Mental Therapy Adjustments									
Other Issues (define)									
New Information									
Physician's Signature: This form must be signed by the Physician	Total								

Monitoring and Review of Health and Safety at Work

Health and Safety Executives recommend that policies and procedures on health and safety be monitored and reviewed periodically, at least annually. It is recommended that employers monitor the rate of accidents and incidents at work to see if it is going up or down. It is recommended that employers talk to their staff to know what is happening at work, and this will help them to review the policies and procedures, so as to minimise risks. Control measures must be checked to see how (if) they are working. Assessments must be reviewed in case things have changed, and record the significant findings with the risk assessment documents. Nothing is constant and managers must review assessments according to changes, either individual service user, the environment, the location, or generally as periodic risk assessment review. This will help to identify where things have improved or deteriorated. Staff must be encouraged to record their findings, observations, incidents and accidents on a regular basis. In addition, monitoring and review can be achieved through the following:

> ➢ Audits of Risks
> ➢ Review of Practices

> ➤ Active Monitoring
> ➤ Learning from Experience
> ➤ Reactive Monitoring
> ➤ Updating of policies and procedures

Types of Monitoring

There are two types of monitoring of health and safety at work, namely, active and reactive.

Active Method is the monitoring the design, the development, the installation and operation of risk management systems at workplace. This method is a preventive measure such as routine inspections of RIDDOR, COSHH, PPE, MHOR, PUWER, and other likely incidents or accidents on the part of the service user's health, care plan, the premises, surveillance, medication, and the environment. All these must be monitored regularly for any changes. There must be effective communication by recording and verbal reports.

Reactive Method is a corrective measure taken after health and safety have been breached. This system monitors poor health and safety procedures and practices that led to an incident or accident. However, this method of monitoring maybe mandatorily imposed by the CQC or HSE as an action plan to ensure that such incidents may not occur again. This normally looks into the review of policies and procedures.

To monitor health and safety at work properly, there must be pre-determined measures. There must be performance checks to make sure that it conforms to the determined measures. There must be appraisal (review) on all systems. Policies and procedures must be followed by inductions and training of staff on how to use, monitor and report anything suspicious relating to the health and safety systems.

Working in Partnership

Partnership working is the key to achieve good practice and customer satisfaction in healthcare sector. For effective monitoring of care services, Care Quality Commission (CQC) works in partnership with other organisations such as NHS England, adass, Ofsted, Healthwatch England, and others. Care Service providers are required to work in partnership with other stakeholders, so as to achieve the principles of person-centred care. Working in partnership for the benefits of care users includes the carers, the GP, the pharmacist, the physio-therapist, the nutritionist, the social workers, the district nurse, the advocate, the police, etc., and others depending on the health condition of the service user. Partnership working enables holistic approach to care, and to share information about service, to improve the overseeing of care, to share the advantages of joint resources and activities, and most importantly, to reduce or remove duplications.

Partnership Working, Care Plan and the Service Users

Regulation 9 of the Care Standards is person-centred care. Planning for care for an individual is focused primarily on his or her needs. This also calls for co-operation amongst all the stakeholders in working together to agree on the best possible care for the care user. Typical care users include: dementia, mental health conditions, eating disorders, learning disability, physical disabilities, sensory impairments, substance misuse problems, caring for adults under 65 years old, and adults over 65 years old. Depending on the health condition of a service user, the care plan will include the inputs of all the stakeholders. The needs of the care user must be assessed collectively, so as to put together the best possible care plan.

Care Users

Dementia
Mental Disorder
Eating Disorder
Learning Disability
Physical Disability
Sensory Impairment
Substance Misuse
The Elderly

Coronavirus (COVID-19) Pandemic: Information for Providers

The Health Protection (Coronavirus) Regulations 2020

CQC stated that "we're making changes to the way we work during the coronavirus (COVID-19) pandemic. They include how we do our job and support providers to keep people safe. They also affect how people communicate with us, or send us applications or information."

(Care Quality Commission 2020 (Coronavirus Act 2020)

Access Information at: https://www.cqc.org.uk/guidance-providers/all-services/coronavirus-covid-19-pandemic-information-providers

Notification	Registered providers must notify us about certain changes, events and incidents that affect their service or the people who use it. • Death of any person using the service • Death of detained mental health patient • Dental care services: Closure and reduction of service

Registration	A COVID-19 registration is any application from a health or social care provider where you: • Intend to deliver services which provide additional health and social care capacity in an area • Contribute to the control of the outbreak of coronavirus or the treatment of people who have contracted the illness • DHSC Response to COVID19 • https://www.cqc.org.uk/guidance-providers/registration/covid-19-registrations
Running your service and providing care	CQC Emergency Support Framework is not an inspection, and we are not rating your performance: • DBS and other recruitment checks • Working within the Mental Capacity Act during the coronavirus pandemic • Innovation and good practice in response coronavirus (COVID-19) • https://www.cqc.org.uk/guidance-providers/how-we-inspect-regulate/emergency-support-framework-what-expect

Contacting CQC	**Mental health services:** please support patients to use online services to communicate with us https://www.cqc.org.uk/contact-us https://www.cqc.org.uk/notifications 03000616161 enquiries@cqc.org.uk

Ownership Declaration

This book will help you to find relevant information relating to the provision of healthcare services quickly. It is made user-friendly and enables health practitioners to relate with their service user effectively to ensure patient satisfaction.

In case this book is misplaced, if found please return to:

This book belongs to: _________________________________

Contact details: ____________________________________

Telephone: ____

For the promotion of good practice, we thank you for returning this book to the rightful owner.

Useful Information

1. Health and Social Care Act 2008 (Regulated Activities) Regulations 2014
2. Health and Social Care Regulations 2018
3. Care Act 2014
4. Health Protection (Coronavirus) Regulations 2020
5. Coronavirus Act 2020
6. Health and Safety at Work Act 1974
7. Management of Health and Safety at Work Regulations 1999
8. Safety Representatives and Safety Committees Regulations 1997
9. Data Protection Act 1998
10. Equality Act 2010
11. Human Rights Act 1998
12. Safeguarding Vulnerable Group Act 2006
13. Health and Safety (Fire Aid) Regulations 1981
14. International Development (Gender Equality) Act 2014
15. Freedom of Information Act 2005

16. Care Quality Commission (Registration) Regulations 2009

17. Control of Substances Hazardous to Health (COSHH) Regulations 2002

18. Reporting of Injuries, Diseases and Dangerous Occurrences Regulations (RIDDOR) 1995

19. Disclosure of Barring Services (DBS) established by Police Act 1997 (Criminal Records) (Registration) Regulations 2006

20. Provision and Use of Work Equipment Regulations (PUWER) 1998

21. The Work Place (Health, Safety and Welfare) Regulations 1992

22. Manual Handling Operations Regulations 1992

23. Lifting Operations and Lifting Equipment Regulations (LOLER) 1998

24. The Regulatory Reform (Fire Safety) Order (RRO) 2005

25. Personal Protective Equipment at Work (PPE) Regulations 1992

26. Raelin, J. (2008) Work-Based Learning: Bridging Knowledge and Action in the Workplace

27. Skills for Care (2015) Common Core Principles to Support Self-care, second edition

28. National Institute for Health and Care Excellence (2014) Putting NICE guidance into practice

29. Department of Health (2013) Controlled Drugs (Supervision of Management and Use)
30. Centre for Policy on Ageing (2012) Managing and Administering Medication in Care Home for Older People
31. Fire Safety Regulations in non-domestic premises (2010)
32. Department of Health (2013) Transforming Care: A national response to Winterbourne View Hospital (Final Report)
33. Sir Robert Francis Report (2013) Report on the Mid-Staffordshire NHS Foundation Trust Public Inquiry
34. National Advisory Group on the Safety of Patients in England (2013) Improving the Safety of Patients in England
35. Care Quality Commission (2015) Plan Care, Putney Inspection Report
36. Care Quality Commission (Directors of Adult Social Services (adass, 2011) A protocol between CQC and Councils with social services responsibilities
37. Tandon and Trinh-Shevrin (2010) Understanding Patient and Stakeholder Engagement in Patient Centred Outcomes Research
38. Adrian Sieff (2012) The Health Foundation, Working in Partnership to Deliver Patient-centred

39. Health and Safety Executive (HSE) Personal Protective Equipment (PPE) at Work Regulations 1992

40. Office of the Public Guardian (2013) Safeguarding Policy

41. HNS England (2014) Confidentiality Policy

42. Department of Health (2003) Confidentiality NHS Code of Practice

43. Health and Social Care Information Centre (HSCIC, 2013) A Guide to Confidentiality in Health and Social Care

44. Care Quality Commission (2010) Guidance about compliance; summary of regulations, outcomes and judgement framework

45. Nursing and Midwifery Council (NMC, 2015) The Code, Standards of Practice and Behaviour for Nurses and Midwives

46. General Social Care Council (GSCC, 2010) Codes of Practice for Social Care Workers

47. Care Quality Commission (2015) A fresh start for the regulation and inspection of adult social care, working together to change how we inspect and regulate adult social care services

48. Coronavirus (COVID-19) Pandemic: Information for Providers: Available at: https://www.cqc.org.uk/guidance-providers/all-services/

coronavirus-covid-19-pandemic-information-providers (Accessed 30/7/2020)

49. The Health Protection (Coronavirus) Regulations 2020: available at: https://www.gov.uk/government/news/health-secretary-announces-strengthened-legal-powers-to-bolster-public-health-protections-against-coronavirus (accessed 20/7/2020)

50. Egam (1975) The Skilled Helper Model

51. Argyle (1972) Communication Cycle

52. Wayne Booth (1961) The Rhetoric of Fiction: Explores the consequences of bad rhetoric

53. Piaget (1977) Cognitive Structures

54. Bandura (1977) Social Learning theory

www.ingramcontent.com/pod-product-compliance
Lightning Source LLC
Chambersburg PA
CBHW051457250726
48655CB00001B/460